# ROOSTER'S CAGE

A true story of one teen's survival

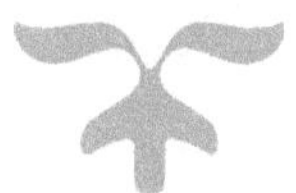

Thank You to the love of my life, my husband Andy, ,

my amazing friends, Ray & Laurie,  and my Counselor Donna for  having my six.

# CHAPTER 1

## *Inappropriate*

My story starts out when I'm 43, and just moved in with the man I plan to marry. My son is 11, almost 12, and has already started showing signs of puberty. My fiancé is 48 and amazing. He is so loving, and caring, and still tough at the same time. I didn't understand what was happening. The nightmares were getting worse and worse. I've always had them, but not as real as they were becoming. Being sexually used or thrown around like a rag doll. They were really getting to me. I see no faces, just the acts themselves. Since we moved in, they are nightly and starting to get to me mentally during the day. The crying, the anxiety, the panic attacks. There were rooms and furniture I was AFRAID of and couldn't remember why I was afraid, I just knew that I was. I began withdrawing into myself, avoiding people and putting space in between my fiancé and myself.

I was terrified and withdrawn.

Sitting together, one day, my fiancé asks me "Who molested you? "I didn't know what to say, I've always denied it, but a part of me couldn't this day. Then he asks, "was it your father or stepfather?" I froze. I remember being too close to my step father, but not much else. I started to shake, and then the flashbacks began. Over a series of days, then weeks. they came. I could be cleaning, or we could be doing something together. Or my fiancé tickling or wrestling with my son and I have an anxiety attack.. why? He's never given me reason to think otherwise, then the flashbacks began…

Every family has secrets, right?

This is mine. I've carried it around for almost 30 years.

I was 15, and nobody wanted me. At least, that's how I felt.

I grew up in a complex family environment. My mother was a single mother as far back as I could remember. I vaguely remember my oldest sister being with us, she was 10 years older than I was. I do remember my middle sister, growing up with her, she often cared for me when we were alone. My mother, either working or off meeting the next "Mr. Right" in her life. Life changed after my middle sister was married. I was already an Aunt to my oldest sister's daughter. Our mother, not ever being that hands-on mother, found me a challenge to handle. I was loud, full of energy and stubborn. By 12, I was sent to live with my Father and his wife. Shortly after, my mother married the man who I would come to know as 'Dad', but everyone else just called him *Rooster.*

There, I was a handful, and did not receive the attention I desired. Called names, fights, and more aggression over the next 3 years.  It was the summer before my 15th birthday, I came to visit my mother for the summer, like I had for the previous three years. She boasted of the local college and its music program in hopes that I would gravitate toward attending college there.

Her and I had never seen eye to eye. My sister closest in age to me was the child who (I felt) could do no wrong. She had found the love of her life and married at 16. She used to try and tell me how special I was because I was born despite her use of contraceptives. I just heard that I was her mistake.

My birth father on the other hand, was conflicted. He seemed lost in another world. A world filled with hand made radios, and other people around the world.

Neither parent had time for me or my interests.

My mother had married multiple times, but this marriage different. She was very adamant that 'this one' worked.  My step father, worked for a county jail when they married, and had since then, moved my mother and himself up North, where I visited that summer. Well, it started that summer.

They lived on a hobby farm. That is, a farm that was not the primary financial income. My step Dad, Rooster, worked for a factory as well. I loved animals. I understood them so much more than humans. At the time, the only thing they raised were rabbits and chickens. There was so much to do on a farm, and he was so nice to me. I was excited, that I was able to play with the baby bunnies and help. I wasn't sure where I fit in there, but I did enjoy it. I spent the summer attending farm shows, county fairs, and local events.  She had been married to him for most of the time I'd lived with my biological father, so he wasn't a stranger, but this created an opportunity to get to know him better.

By the end of the summer, I wasn't sure I wanted to go back, but I did. Helping to clean out cages, had earned me my own bunny, that I named "Baby". Mostly because every day I went out to the pen, I'd say 'How's the babies today'? and this one would step forward to be pet.  I'd grown so attached that I cleaned cages, watered and fed them daily to allow me to keep it.  This time, I was put on a bus, rather than flying, mostly I think because of my bunny. I think I'd been back three months, when I heard a heated phone conversation about who was getting "stuck" with me.

I was devastated. Didn't anyone want me?  After hearing the same conversation from that side as well as hearing Rooster have that conversation with my mother and his charming way of telling me neither my father or mother wanted me, I had come to the conclusion that he  was the only one who was arguing to keep me.  I had decided.. I wanted to go back. I was warned that there was no going back if I did this, and would have to leave my rabbit behind should I decide to do so.  So, another week later, I was shipped back to the farm.  Changing schools was a challenge too. I'd gone from a large school to a small local central school. In my previous school, there were more in my homeroom than there were in my grade in the local school. Still, I thought it was nice to be able to walk to school, and the work was easier.

My favorite part was that since it was a central school, I could fill my study halls with tutoring for the Elementary classes, or helping out with the preschoolers lunch program. I really thought this was how it was 'supposed' to be. I saw friends and other families that I thought seemed normal, and so badly wanted that. That year, to help me improve my self-esteem, my Rooster took me to Erie and we signed up for a modeling program through JRP modeling school. I learned about presentation, hair, makeup, nutrition and began doing commercials, boat shows and a calendar. In my naivety, I did not retain any rights to use. At the time, I did not care. I was so empowered by feeling beautiful, I began to believe it brought things to me. As my body progressed into womanhood, I was both romanticizing and fearing the progression of my body. Rooster, rapidly took on the role of a dad, or what I *thought* was the role of a dad. We worked in the barn together, talked about almost everything, and I tried to spend as much time as I could with him.

I was spoiled. He bought me gifts, and talked to me about the animals, taught me how to raise them, and walked me through relationships and life issues. I had a family. Everyone we ran into mistook me for being his daughter. Roots, small town, animals, it was all euphoric to a child who never knew what family was like prior to that. Who wouldn't bend their own personal boundaries to keep their image of a personal lottery?

My mother, no longer had to work at that point. She enjoyed keeping the paperwork done. I was always in awe of how organized she was, and that she made the best dumplings, (still does) but our home was never clean. I learned to clean things properly, and Dad would give me money for it. For the first time, I had my own money. We grew closer and closer the more we worked together on the farm.

I remember moving in October, shortly after my 15th birthday, and by the end of the year, I was sitting in the recliner with him. Being an old house, and the living room under construction, we often had to sit under blankets to stay warm.

Sundays we watched westerns together, and hardly moved. Even as old as I was, I felt like I missed out on being a 'little girl' and became dubbed a "daddy's girl". I was showered with gifts, or taken places. Many Fridays, he and I would go to a fish fry together. I asked why mom didn't go, he told me that she didn't care for fish. I found out later that was not so.

Things started to progress, comfort levels, relaxed personal boundaries. Started simple, Rooster would wear his underwear downstairs, mom in her nightshirt, I still wore pj's. Rooster would hug me, and put his hand under my shirt. I'd never had a dad, is this normal? Must be, right?

It was never discussed what personal boundaries are supposed to be, and even as an adult, I had issues with this dating, and even friendship boundaries. I've always wanted to make people happy, don't we all?

My modeling career progressed, and eventually the calendar was shot, as well as some proofs. Rooster convinced me I should take some extras at home to add to my portfolio. It will seem like I'm more experienced than I am if I have some varied shots included. I was excited. Modeling? I was the pizza faced, coke bottle glasses girl, that was picked on from the time I was 7. I jumped on the idea.

The day of the shoot, I picked out my clothes with precision. I knew my best features, So I geared the outfits to show them off. He was always telling me I was beautiful, but that day, I felt like a top model! Little did I know, but I would have something in common with her that day. We packed up the clothes, I did my hair and makeup and headed out to the back of the field. I was always so clumsy. I dumped stuff over, spilled stuff on me, but still had a lot of fun. Since we all ran around in underwear at home, I wasn't super nervous about changing. He'd made a point that my bathing suits showed more than underwear does.  Still, I was uneasy and didn't know why.  I would always turn around, it didn't feel right. I thought I was just being modest. The last outfit was a button down black cotton dress with a V neck.  We took a few pictures with it, but my bra kept showing through.  He convinced me that we should try it with no bra. So, I unbuttoned what I needed, and pulled the straps through the arms, and then unclipped the back, pulling it through the front.  At that point, I was very uneasy.  I was trusting him, with my safety, and my virtue.  I was not photographing well, due to my nervousness. He said it looked good, but maybe I should unbutton one or two to make it sexier.  I didn't want to be sexier, I wanted the cover girl modeling stuff, not the body or runway stuff. I did it anyway, what harm could it do? I was still covered up. Over the course of a full roll of film, and some adjusting his manhood  on his part, I wasn't getting any more comfortable and asked to wrap up and if we had enough. I did not know that would be a prelude, but I was in no mood to have a conversation on the way back to the house.

Later, after the film developed, I noticed that  my nipple showed, in not just one, but multiple photos. He assured me that both the photos and negatives would be destroyed. I was mortified. For weeks , I found it a challenge to sit on his lap, and be alone with him, but I was.  To my dismay, my mother avoided us.

It started with rubbing.. under my shirt.. then higher.  Months went by and he inched his way up to my breast area. At first, I jumped, and would push his hand away, but he would be very unpleasant and I was fearful of disappointing him.

By the following summer, he had inched his way in to the edge of my underwear and up to  my nipple area.

My mother smoked, I would stand in the garage and talk to her, or sit behind her since she kept the garage door cracked.  I asked her if I was being silly with all the affection he was giving, she said I was, and was just not used to receiving it.  That was my education session, I shrugged it all off and continued to enjoy the family that was emerging in our future. I didn't go into detail. Another summer rolled around. Filled with Hay baling, stacking and chores. County fairs and other summer entertainment. I grew closer and closer to my new father figure. That birthday, was my sweet 16, and I received a suede green western jacket with fringes. (Don't laugh, this was 1990 and it was super trendy then) I knew they were expensive, and I was giddy with excitement. It wasn't long after that, while watching TV, laying with him in the recliner under a blanket, that the touching went a little farther... north and south. His hand made its way into my underwear,

It still wasn't all the way there, but it was close.  I pushed his hand away and didn't know what to do. The more we sat together, the more my mother seemed to approve.  All winter long we sat together, then one evening, he pushed his finger into my vaginal cavity. I jumped! He told me to relax, and he rubbed around the area for the remainder of the evening. We always sat with a blanket covering what he was doing.  I tried to avoid him, but he became angry. As I kid, I felt trapped. What do I do? Am I over reacting? Was it just a loving fatherly touch? Was there something wrong with it? How do I tell?

I couldn't do much more than cry myself to sleep.

We often went on walks. I would let him know how serious it was by how far we had to go. For example, if it was an easy thing, then I'd ask to talk in the barn. If it was a normal issue, but a bit more serious, then we would take a walk around the block, but if it was really serious, it was a beach talk.

This was a beach talk. After hearing from my mother, that I over react, I thought it best to talk to dad. I asked him about it. Was it intentional? Was it accidental? He asked me instead to decide, and asked me if I wanted to know what to do with a boy when the time came. What to do and what not to do, and how to get out of sex if I needed to.  It begun there. I asked him why he was doing that, touching me. He said he loved me and wanted to teach me what to do with a man. Didn't I want to get married and know what to do? This is part of the role of being a father. I wanted to get married, and have a big family. Didn't I? I decided that I did, and allowed the progression.

Over the next progressive weeks, I was guided how to handle his male parts, and he progressed into unchartered territory.  I was both confused, and scared. I didn't know who to tell, what to do, or how to handle it. He would guide my hand over his penis and hold it there, rubbing it until he was satisfied. The first time he 'came' I was mortified.  I knew not to raise a fuss over it, because the consequence was his anger spiraling out of control.

I was always walking on eggshells. Me and mom both. I knew he loved mom, and wouldn't hurt her, but when he got angry, I was the one with the bruises, sore arms or worse.

I then had a choice to make, do I fight to go back to my 'real' father, and face being locked upstairs of their house, separated to keep me from ruining his family? Leaving the only semblance of a family I felt I ever had? Or stay, keep him satiated and be happier?

At first, it was just touching, and I sucked up the shame, and hurt.  Somehow, I managed to turn myself off when he was satisfying himself. Thinking of other things, Getting lost in daydreams and in the cavity of my own mind. By my senior year in high school, we were sneaking around for full intercourse. I learned how to shut off my feelings, to turn my focus off.  If he sat down, it was always in a corner, and I would lean on him or stand next to him. His hand would at first touch my legs, then slide up to my underwear, to run his finger along my vaginal cavity. If I pulled back, he would be angry, and I would receive the wrath of his anger over something much smaller later.  I felt guilty, like I was doing something wrong. He was cheating on my mother, wasn't he? Do other fathers that spoil their daughters have this kind of relationship? Some part of me.  knew it didn't feel right, but how could I stop it? What do I do? I asked for a walk and told him I didn't want to anymore. The lesson had been learned, and I didn't want to.  He said ok but could hear it was painstaking to say it.

The next week was tough. Rooster's anger was on a level I hadn't seen before.  I made him angry, and he made sure I suffered. I was restricted from friends, from anyone else we knew.  On one such evening, I was being defiant, I'd stopped the sex, I'd stopped the touching, and I didn't want to go back. I felt empowered. I refused to do something that he told me to do, even today, it escapes me what I refused, but the outcome will forever be etched in my mind.  He grabbed me by the neck and pushed me to my room. I tried to close the door, and he pulled it open. He then grabbed my shirt, pulled then pushed me by my shirt, I fell and hit the closet door. The events up to that point had ripped my shirt, and a necklace someone had given me. I sat and cried. What do I do? I can't live like this. I had to ask permission to use the phone, we had no computer, and we rarely went anywhere. I no longer visited my father and wasn't allowed sleepovers of any kind.  I was scared.

One more year, one more year, I just kept telling myself. After two weeks of his anger, my mother came to me and asked what has gotten into me. She wanted to know why I "all of a sudden" decided I was out to make things harder on myself.

I gave in.

What else was there?

The second week, before giving in, I went to the guidance counselors at school. Sat down with him and told him that my step father had a horrible temper and that I was scared. That he was violating me... After all, they were there because they wanted to help kids, right? That they would protect me, call the police, my father, somebody, right?  They didn't call my mother, they called

Rooster.  When he picked me up, he told them we were having problems at home, and this was probably to get back at him for punishing me… and took me back home.

My mother was angry with me for telling lies that could have gotten him into trouble.  What was SHE supposed to do? When I graduate in a few years, she'll be lonely. Did I want that? Why was I punishing her?

That's it, I was trapped.

I spent my senior year, in submission to this man. I vowed that my body would not ever be used like that when I left home.  My graduation was in June, I was 17. I'd only been allowed to date minimally, so I never found my hero to rescue me. It was up to me. Instead, I rode it out until I got a good job that would move me. That following spring, not quite a year later, I packed my truck and moved.

My mother told me I broke his heart.

*Why tell My tale now?*

In my life, I am engaged to a wonderful, loving, protective, amazing man.  This secret has haunted me for nearly 30 years.  It's been easy to hide it, there was only he and I that knew. One afternoon, while we were dating, my fiancé sat me up and asked me "Who molested you? ", I was speechless. I'd didn't know what to say. I'd been asked in the past, but denied it, or avoided answering.

This has affected every relationship I've ever had. As I grew, I realized how *inappropriate* this was, I was a girlfriend to him, not a daughter.

Even more important, I have a son. This all started over us moving in together and planning a yearly visit to my parents.  My husband is the same age as my step father, myself the same age as my mother, and my son the same age as I was.

This became a trigger. Nightmares, stress, and a myriad of other issues.

To discover if I was the only one, 3yrs prior I contacted his children. I always wondered why he didn't have contact with them.

His son talked about the mental and physical abuse, his daughter, an eerily similar situation. It was a story of mental, physical, sexual, emotional and financial abuse.

**It was easy to hide it when nobody knew.**

Even worse, I chose men like that my whole life. My son's father was physically, mentally, sexually and financially abusive.  I thought I could hide it, that I could bury it and not let it affect me. It became like an infection that never went away.

I didn't come forward again until I was 43 with a family of my own. My husband said he just knew, one day together, he asked me outright "Who molested you?". I was dumfounded, I had been able to hide it all my life. How did he know? I finally confessed. It came out in a flood of tears. Shaking, and crying, it was a relief that someone else knew.

I still have issues with recliners, sleeping and my sexuality. Recently, I sent a letter to my stepfather that my fiancé knew, and another to my mother telling her that My Son would not be visiting them. She was welcome any time.  It will be hard to be seen like that by my family, and friends. I've always been scared to tell my story. I feared my son would find out what someone did to his mother. How I would be looked at or rejected? So much shame in myself for 'allowing' the abuse. So much shame in the secret.

Perspective can always rationalize any situation, we all see things differently.

CHAPTER 2

*Mind Games*

How does it get so far that one person is able to manipulate someone to a point they allow them to abuse them physically, financially, sexually or emotionally?

He was very charming. Knew just how to mentally groom someone and manipulate them to his own choice. This is someone prominent in the community, amongst well known in town, in the county... how exactly does a teen of 15 compete with that? Who would believe a 'troubled teen' that this was happening from such an 'upstanding' man. He knew how to talk to someone and sell them on anything. He was an amazing salesman, even beyond reason. He could make anything sound like it was awful if it didn't come from him.

How easy is it to control an attention starved teen coming from a home with someone who was alcoholic and struggling with severe PTSD? I wanted attention, he made sure I knew no one wanted me but him. That I knew about the fights with my birth father, and my mother. That they argued against wanting me in their home. That I would "infect" whoever I was near? Even to the point of making up a story about meeting me before my mother married my birth father, and that I could be his, so it was ok.

On one such occasion, early in the grooming stage, before I came to live there, I begged to keep a rabbit. He raised them to auction locally. The Amish ate the meat. He gave me some conditions that were easily met, to gain favor with me, and let me keep a rabbit. I was able to save one life. It went back home with me at the end of summer. It worked, by the end of summer, I was convinced no one wanted me but him.

Once I was shipped back, I felt I was out of place. I asked to go back. They let me. I never saw my birth father again. Nor did he hear my forgiveness. I told him it was God's forgiveness he needed.

I kept up with my little brother through a friend close by.

Once I was sent back, he would take me places and buy me things. Especially when he lost his temper or pushed farther than I wanted. He always apologized with things, and often came home with 'something special'. I felt showered. Most teen would have loved it, but I knew if there was a gift, there was also a price I was paying for it somewhere else. Over my lifetime, I found myself shying away from any men bearing gifts. I found it very difficult to accept a gift. When I married my son's father, that became prevalent in my marriage. I was ok not receiving Christmas Gifts, if it meant I wasn't expected to have sex with him. Most men I dated were avoided if they brought gifts. I was ok receiving them from women, but never from men. Still to this day, I find my guard jumping up if I receive a gift from my husband.

On one occasion, when I was 16, I tried to tell the counselor. *I tried* being the key phrase. I told him I was being 'touched'. I was being handled... inappropriately. I was mortified when Rooster showed up instead of my mother. The guidance counselor, with no way to tell if I was lying or telling the truth, called my "parents". I found out later, only my step father was talked to. My mother, never having received the call, never knew I tried to reach out.

Our past will often inadvertently carve our future. It will damage future relationships if we don't deal with the damage it creates in our soul.

By the time I was 16, I was brainwashed into thinking I was alone and trapped. I would plan how much I would need to be on my own, and plan what I would take. I worked toward a vehicle, thinking that was my freedom from prison. I was stuck. I couldn't buy a car without a job and couldn't get a job for a payment until I was working.  Once I was working, I thought I would be able to save enough to get away. Unfortunately, the vehicle I had was not so compliant. Over the next year, the vehicle cost me more than I could make with two jobs, but at least I was out of the house and working. Home only for a couple hours at a time. Giving me an opportunity to date. I chose large men, the bad-boy type that I thought would rescue me from my situation. That was not my happy ending either. So, I took a job working WITH him, using his good name as a rider to get a really good job. I jumped on the first chance to get away. I was almost 19 by then.

So desperate for someone to save me, I looked for that tough guy, someone who would fight for me. Instead, found myself dating the bad-boys. The first, I found in bed with someone else, the next, a little tougher.  On a date, watching a movie at his house, without his mother there, we started watching a movie. Mountain Dew, and pizza, nothing fantastic, but something was different. I started to feel as though I was drinking... a buzz. Maybe that's what euphoria is, right? That feeling of being there, but not there. By half way through the movie, I felt like I was sleepy. I still don't remember some of the details, just the nightmares that followed. Of me being rolled over and my pants pulled down. Paralyzed, can't move.  I felt everything, him forcing himself inside me and finishing. Wiping me off and pulling my pants off. I thought I napped. The nightmares haunting me for years.

I bounced from boyfriend, each time trapped, controlled and sometimes, even pregnant. Each time I tried to start over, I carried the secret with me. Not just damaging to me, but to everyone around me. The only comfort was a dog, Jiggs, that I'd rescued. A Boston Terrier with a heart of gold. He was damaged emotionally and physically, just as I was. Found him in a field, shortly after leaving. For 7 years, he was the only love I knew. He was with me for 4 of my miscarriages. After him, came another, Tristan, another Boston Terrier, that stayed with me until I was in my 40s. The only form of love I knew other than children.

When I moved, I was reunited with a guy I'd known in my teens.  The medication dulling any senses I had. I viewed it logically. He was a farmer. He was striving for his own Dairy farm and was in the middle of buying his own house and land. He appeared to be everything I wanted. The shiny penny. I would marry him and raise a family on a farm. Have my animals and have a man that would protect me. He rarely gave gifts and was always the model boyfriend. Later I found out that they referred to that as "dating games" and laughed about the 'gold handcuff' (pointing to the gold rings on their fingers)

I never felt safe.

For 4 years we tried, the secret always with me. Secrets of his own, within his family that I never knew, but they rotted away our marriage over the few years together. Each time my father-in-law left town, he was the man I married. Home for breakfast, lunch and dinner, sweet, and easy to be around. I knew within the hour. Mostly, though, he wasn't like that. Family secrets and holds on each other, pried us apart each day until again, I had a marriage with separate lives, only this time, I was the mental, verbal, physical and financial prisoner. Each time something would happen with the family, I was the one who received the other end. My son and I were "burdens", "worth less than the cows". Our car would only start when he wanted us to go somewhere. (I found out later, the spark plugs were being pulled) Out of food, he would go to his parents. I would hide food for the baby, for emergencies. I eventually had to call Rooster for help. The baby was sick and on quarantine. Again, trapped in a prison. Gilded as it may be.  I sold the animals, hid money, worked in private and after realizing that the abuse would be passed down to our child, as it had passed to him, I left.

Until I was older, and with a man that loved me for me, not what my body could give him. My body, riddled with scars from Cancer treatments and surgeries, could not give what I could in the past. His patience and love were beyond words and formed a bond that was enough to make me feel safe.

Then I told. The nightmares, the flashbacks, the horror, all flooded back. I felt like was repeating my mother's mistakes. Man, after man, then when my son is 12, I'm in my 40's and my husband in his 40's, all over again. Was I making a mistake? It came out. First to my husband, unprompted, he asked the fateful question. "Who molested you?" I didn't reply my usual knee-jerk response of laughing it off. Never truly answering it. I said nothing. I did nothing. Stunned I asked, "What would make you ask that?"

He had put pieces over the years we had known each other. Little things that I said or did. He dreamt that something similar had happened. Once we moved in, it all came flooding back. I told him and started counseling.

Next was my sister, then finally, my mother. Each person I told, less of the shame was on me, and transferred to the person that it belonged too.

Rooster.

For all his charm, and fear, he was nothing but a dirty old man now. Waiting to die.

My struggle wasn't over though. My mother, left confused with a heartbroken abuser, was no fun time either. I thought by keeping my mouth shut about what happened would secure a future for her as she grew old. Instead, it fostered a prison from which she was later trapped.  It has affected every relationship I've ever had.  Every boyfriend, every girl-friend, every co-worker. I always wondered what they were hiding, lying about, what was going on that they were keeping secrets. Does anyone need help? Can I help someone else?

My mother called tonight. Another attempt to protect me and bury this. Advised me that his first daughter tried to take it to court, and it didn't go anywhere. That I could tell my fiancé where he was, so that he could finish him off. I know I can no longer litigate or extradite. I also know he has people he can hide with. Hide himself, his secrets. No, no courts here, just the rest of the world, in hopes someone else doesn't go through what I have. So, no one else sits, for three years, thinking they are alone, and helpless. So, no one else, becomes just another victim.

I hope by reading this, you, whoever you are, know there IS help. FREE.  Nationwide and caring.

# CHAPTER 3

## *Escape*

planned my escape for over two years. How much money I would need, that I would need a car. I scanned for apartments while I was working, avoiding the house. Sometimes slept in my car to avoid coming home to the house I saw as my own prison

I was once told, the Devil doesn't imprison us, we imprison ourselves. He puts shiny things inside the cage. Make's it what we think we need to have, and before we know it, we have closed the door to the cage ourselves because we are comfortable in it. Much like a bird that has its cage door and does not leave out of fear.

Some cages are more gilded than others, but cages they are. Being an animal lover, I spend the first two years, enveloped in the small barn of animals we kept. I loved being in the barn. Horses, cattle, rabbits and of course, chickens and fighting roosters. I had a nice room, the barn and was constantly receiving gifts. I had my own gilded cage. I wanted freedom. I sought it for most of the imprisonment I planned my escape and when the cage door was open, I fled. I was not free, not yet.

Outside the cage was proving more difficult than I imagined, but at least I was free of the abuse. Or at least, I thought I was. I moved on, dating man after man who sought me for my body, physical attraction being the most sought-after commodity in our 20's. I hated it. I loved modeling in my teens, but as I grew, I no longer wanted my body sought after. I declined an offer from the city because part of the contract stated nude photos or partial nudity was to be accepted. I jumped from boyfriend to boyfriend, looking for that hero, only to turn to myself. Not much of a hero, I chose a man for my first marriage who slept next to me a year later and had yet to be forward physically. I convinced myself that he was just being a gentleman. We were married, and often did not sleep on the same floor or in the same bed together. He was safe.

I turned to my faith. I knew a part of me was broken. That I needed to heal. I found a church that was very forward thinking and had a woman minister. Being raised Catholic, that was unheard of. It was a non-denominational church, that talked of healing, and peace. The goodness of God. I was drawn in. I was already a faithful follower when I met the man I was marrying so we were married there. I continued to travel there even when we moved farther away. I enjoyed the healing messages.

That's when it started. I gave my life to Christ, the seed my grandmother planted when I was young, the seed of faith started to grow. Each person is different, it grows slowly for some, others it sprouts. At this time, it sprouted. I felt like I was healing.

Four years later, my faith, and my marriage, damaged beyond repair. My husband and I had separate lives and unable to bring it together. Starting over for the second time in my life was no picnic. We each had placated our needs in spending. 'keeping up with the Jones' was an expensive path.  Wiping out and starting over I started a new love, that I thought was my soul mate. We were perfect.

He was wild and free from anyone's grasp.

Funny how a perspective can change the image. Free he was not. With three children to two different women and his mother holding his finances, he had toys, but they belonged to everyone else. He submitted to their will choosing his things over love, and I was shattered yet again. Just as 9/11 was airing on the news, so was my own tragedy. I was losing a baby, out of wedlock to a miscarriage, and an accident took my beloved dog that had been my companion since the summer I moved out. I was devastated. I lost my house, my car, my baby and my fur-baby all in the same weekend. Like a bad country music song, I was living day to day.

Starting over that time was harder. Medicine came into effect, placating my flashbacks, and everything else that mattered. I tried to get this man back, only to fall deeper into a hole, I had a hard time crawling back out of.  By the week between Christmas and New Year, I was done.

I sat there with a .22 pistol in my hand, that took the life of my dog and thought how quick he died. My phone rings, my friend Neta on the other end. "you have to come to my house please? Now? "When I ask why, she tells me she will talk to me when I get there. When I get there, she says "I don't know why, I just felt like I HAD to call you and get you here quick, are you ok?" Exhausted and flabbergasted, I tell her "I'm fine." When all I wanted to do was break down and cry. After spending an afternoon with her, I again go home to my empty house. Well, almost empty, there is a cat hiding somewhere.

The holidays came and went and again, I was in despair, some pills and some alcohol to numb the emotional pain I felt, that made me ache in my bones.  I was awakened by another friend, who came by after trying to reach me on my phone, encouraging me to the bathroom moments before vomiting everything I ingested.

After the new year, I call my boss, and ask to be moved. He calls hours later and tells me where I'm moving. I dropped the phone. It was back to the same area I tried so hard to escape.

God tried to talk to me, I choose not to listen. It was too hard. I wasn't ready. My faith stunted by the events of my life.

My next chapter of my life, I again, turn to regaining control of my life. I had a great job, I had a great boyfriend, and started over, again. This time, with an ex- Army Ranger. PTST again ruling my life. Walking on eggshells that came to a head when I realized I was again trapped. After finding myself pregnant two weeks after having some wine with dinner, I again was losing a baby.  My third to be exact. Trapped with someone who had used my body without my permission.

After writing the first chapter, I wondered if I was doing the right thing by publishing. I was reading a book about being brave enough to expose the secret and healing through it. Opening a long ago wound that I tried to cover and let scab over.

I realized that society ACCEPTS this kind of abuse. Different cultures even encourage the "use" of small children, both male and female. In the news, hundreds of children are still sold in 2018 for sex slavery.

My friend April and I talked about her abuse, and how it was rushed past. She was told that she couldn't litigate, and it was hushed.  Years gone by with a brutal lover, she was kept like a prisoner in her own home, with little health care or support.

Laurie and I talked about her one-time abuse, and meanwhile, my mother texted and called to tell me I would go through a lot of red tape and emotional turmoil for nothing. I know that, if I took him to court. His daughter already tried, years back. But I am not. I am publishing. I will send a signed copy to all his friends. Yes, it may seem a little vindictive, but the chunk of my life this secret has taken, it's a little like pouring peroxide on it. It's an infection that needs cleaned out.

My faith, and my family are both strong now. I have truly escaped from my own prison. I always asked myself what made my story different, why me?  Every story is different, and so is everyone's faith. But in the long run, we are all in this thing called LIFE together.

No matter how you see it. Control, of any kind, is never a loving gesture. It's about power. **THAT** person is ill. get out. Get help.

But most of all. You didn't ask for it or deserve it. Neither did I, at any age.

# Are You Being Abused?

Look over the following questions. Think about how you are being treated and how you treat your partner. Remember, *when one person scares, hurts or continually puts down the other person, it's <u>abuse</u>*.

## Does your partner...
—Embarrass or make fun of you in front of your friends or family?

—Put down your accomplishments or goals?
—Make you feel like you are unable to make decisions?
—Use intimidation or threats to gain compliance?
—Tell you that you are nothing without them?
—Treat you roughly - grab, push, pinch, shove or hit you?
—Call, text, or email you several times a day or show up to make sure you are where you  said you would be?
—Use drugs or alcohol as an excuse for saying hurtful things or abusing you?
—Blame you for how they feel or act?
—Pressure you sexually for things you don't want to do?
—Make you feel like there "is no way out" of the relationship?
—Prevent you from doing things you want - like spending time with your friends or family?
—Try to keep you from leaving after a fight or leave you somewhere after a fight to "teach you a lesson"?

## Do you...
—Sometimes feel scared of how your partner will act?
—Constantly make excuses to other people for your partner's behavior?
—Believe that you can help your partner change if only you changed something about yourself?
—Try not to do anything that would cause conflict or make your partner angry?

—Always do what your partner wants you to do instead of what you want?
—Stay with your partner because you are afraid of what your partner would do if you broke up?

If any of these are happening in your relationship, talk to someone. Without some help, the abuse will continue.

(Adapted from Reading and Teaching Teens to Stop Violence, Nebraska Domestic Violence and S CHECKLIST (provided by the National Coalition Against Domestic Violence) Sexual Assault Coalition, Lincoln, NE). http://www.domesticviolenceinfo.ca/article/questionnaires-153.asp

Please, get help. In the following pages you will find US and International Toll-Free help lines. I encourage you. A note, a call, or use the international symbol, and show it to a caregiver in secret if you fear for you, or a loved one's, safety.

Child Welfare Information Gateway. (2012). Toll-free crisis hotline numbers. Washington, DC: U.S. Department of Health and Human Services, Children's Bureau.

**http://www.childwelfare.** **gov/pubs/reslist/tollfree.cfm** (or) *http://www.childwelfare.gov*

Child Welfare Information Gateway Children's Bureau/ACYF 1250 Maryland Avenue, SW Eighth Floor Washington, DC 20024 800.394.3366 Email: info@childwelfare.gov

*This material may be freely reproduced and distributed.* However, when doing so, please credit Child Welfare Information Gateway.

**Available online at: t http://www.childwelfare. gov/pubs/reslist/tollfree.cfm**

## Toll-Free Crisis Hotline Numbers (USA)

## Child Abuse

Childhelp® Phone: **800.4.A.CHILD (800.422.4453)**
People They Help: Child abuse victims, parents, concerned individuals

## Child Sexual Abuse

Darkness to Light Phone: **866.FOR.LIGHT (866.367.5444)**
People They Help: Children and adults needing local information or resources regarding sexual abuse

## Rape/Incest

Rape, Abuse and Incest National Network (RAINN) Phone: **800.656.HOPE (800.656.4673)** People They Help: Rape and incest victims, media, policymakers, concerned individuals

## Human Trafficking

National Human Trafficking Hotline Phone: **888.373.7888**
People They Help: Victims of human trafficking and those reporting potential trafficking situations People They Help: Individuals, families, professionals

## Missing/Abducted Children

Child Find of America Phone: **800.I.AM.LOST (800.426.5678)** People They Help: Parents reporting lost or abducted children, including parental abductions

Child Find of America—Mediation Phone: **800.A.WAY.OUT (800.292.9688)** People They Help: Parents (abduction, prevention, child custody issues)

National Center for Missing and Exploited Children Phone: **800.THE.LOST (800.843.5678)** TTY: 800.826.7653 People They Help: Families and professionals (social services, law enforcement)

## Youth in Trouble/ Runaways

National Runaway Switchboard Phone: **800.RUNAWAY (800.786.2929)** People They Help: Runaway and homeless youth, families

## Substance Abuse

National Alcohol and Substance Abuse Information Center Phone: **800.784.6776** People They Help: Families, professionals, media, policymakers, concerned individuals

## Family Violence

National Domestic Violence Hotline Phone: **800.799.SAFE (800.799.7233)** TTY: 800.787.3224

Video Phone Only for Deaf Callers: 206.518.9361

People They Help: Children, parents, friends, offenders

## Help for Parents

National Parent Helpline® Phone: **855.4APARENT (855.427.2736)** (available 10 a.m. to 7 p.m., PST, weekdays)

People They Help: Parents and caregivers needing emotional support and links to resources

## Mental Illness

National Alliance on Mental Illness Phone: **800.950.NAMI (800.950.6264)** (available 10 a.m. to 6 p.m., ET, weekdays)

## Suicide Prevention

National Suicide Prevention Lifeline Phone: **800.273.TALK (800.273.8255)** TTY: 800.799.4TTY (800.799.4889) People They Help: Families, concerned individuals

**Disponible en español http://www.childwelfare.gov/ pubs/reslist/sp_tollfree.cfm**

U.S. Department of Health and Human Services Administration for Children and Families Administration on Children, Youth and Families Children's Bureau

Use your smartphone to access this factsheet online.

Child Welfare Information Gateway
Children's Bureau/ACYF
1250 Maryland Avenue, SW
Eighth Floor
Washington, DC 20024
800.394.3366
Email: info@childwelfare.gov
http://www.childwelfare.gov

U.S. Department of Health and Human Services
Administration for Children and Families
Administration on Children, Youth and Families
Children's Bureau

# Toll Free for US and Canada

https://www.childhelp.org/hotline/

*National Child Abuse Hotline* **(1-800) 4-A-Child** *or* **(1-800) 422-4453**

The Childhelp National Child Abuse Hotline is dedicated to the prevention of child abuse.
**Serving the U.S. and Canada**, the hotline is staffed 24 hours a day, 7 days a week with professional crisis counselors who—through interpreters—provide assistance in over 170 languages. The hotline offers crisis intervention, information, and referrals to thousands of emergency, social service, and support resources. All calls are confidential. **Bottom line, we are here to answer the call.**

http://www.nationaldomesticviolencehelpline.org.uk/

24-hour National Domestic Violence Freephone Helpline **0808 2000 247**
Run in partnership between Women's Aid and Refuge

# OTHER INTERNATIONAL HOTLINES

http://www.vachss.com/help_text/hotlines_intl.html

**NSPCC Child Protection Helpline (U.K.)**
Freephone: 0800 800 500
Textphone: 0800 056 0566 (hearing impaired)
Welsh Freephone: 0808 100 2524
Bengali/Sylheti Freephone: 0800 096 7714
Gujarati Freephone: 0800 096 7715
Hindi Freephone: 0800 096 7716
Punjabi Freephone: 0800 096 7717
Urdu Freephone: 0800 096 7718
www.nspcc.org.uk
24-hour service, counseling, advice, referrals for children at risk of abuse and neglect. Report suspected abuse/neglect cases.

**RSPCA (U.K.)**
Phone: 0990 555 999
24-hour cruelty hotline.

**CHILDLINE UK**
Freephone: 0800 11 11
www.childline.org.uk
Free, 24-hour, national helpline for children and youth in trouble or danger throughout the UK.

**CHILDLINE South Africa**
Toll-free: 0800 55555
www.childline.org.za
Toll-free hotline and associated treatment center offers free counseling by phone or in person, for children and youth dealing with physical, sexual, or emotional abuse, and to adult survivors of childhood sexual abuse. The hotline is answered 24 hours a day, 7 days a week.

**HIV/AIDS Hotline South Africa**
Phone: 011 0800 012 322
**HIV/AIDS Hotline Nigeria**
Phone: 01 772 2200 or 01 773 2201

**Kids Help Line (Australia)**
Toll-free: 1-800-55-180024-hour toll-free hotline for children and youth throughout Australia.

**Kids Help Phone (Canada)**
Toll-free: 1-800-668-6868
Canada's only toll-free national hotline for children and youth. Bilingual (English and French).

**Muslim Women's Help Line (U.K.)**
Hotline: 0181 904 8193 or 0181 908 6715
Hotline for Muslim women and girls in the U.K. dealing with domestic violence, sexual abuse, and other problems.

**Action on Elder Abuse (U.K.)**
Freephone: 0808 808 8141
www.elderabuse.org.uk

**National Domestic Violence Hotline (Canada)**
Toll-free: 1-800-363-9010
All provinces. Bilingual (English and French).

**National Eating Disorders Information Centre (Canada)**
Toll-free: 1-866-633-4220

**Nottelefon Zurich**
Phone: 01-291 46 46
www.frauenberatung.ch
(Pages available in German, English, French, Spanish & Italian) Counseling by phone and in person, free referrals to doctors and legal advisors, for women dealing with sexual harassment or abuse, or exploitation by therapists, doctors, ministers, at work or home.

**Women's Aid Federation of England**
Freephone: 0808 2000 247

# INTERNATIONAL HUMAN TRAFFICKING

http://www.vachss.com/help_text/human_trafficking.html#org

**Amnesty International**
322 Eighth Avenue
New York, NY 10001
Phone: (212) 807-8400
www.amnesty.org

**Stop Trafficking**
U.S. Anti-Trafficking Working Group
U.S. Department of State
2001 "C" Street, N.W., Suite 6934
Washington, DC 20520-7512
Phone: (202) 647-5440
secretary.state.gov/www/picw/trafficking/home.htm
Research on human trafficking, U.S. government response, regional initiatives, articles, cases and laws, resources and reference materials.

**Anti-Slavery International**
Thomas Clarkson House
The Stableyard, Broomgrove Road
London SW9 9TL
United Kingdom
Phone: 020 7501 8920
www.antislavery.org
ASI works to abolish "modern slavery," including bonded and forced labor, child labor and commercial sexual exploitation, immigrant trafficking, forced early marriage, and the chattel system.

**Casa Alianza**
Paseo de la reforma 111
Colonia Guerrero
Mexico D.F. 06300
Mexico
www.casa-alianza.org
Casa Alianza is dedicated to the rehabilitation and defense of street children in Latin American countries.

**Solwodi (Solidarity)**
www.solwodi.de
German group dedicated to ending the trafficking of women, and to assisting trafficked women throughout Germany.\

**Counter-Trafficking Service**
International Organization for Migration
17 Route des Moullons
C.P. 71 CH-1211
Geneva 19 Switzerland
Phone: 022 717 9111
https://www.iom.int/cms/en/sites/iom/home.html
Dedicated to assisting trafficked migrants through protection, counseling, free legal and medical services, assisted return and re–integration.

**ECPAT International**
(End Child Prostitution/Pornography and Trafficking)
328 Phayathai Road
Bangkok 10400 Thailand
www.ecpat.net

**Maiti Nepal**
P.O.Box: 9599
Gaushala
Kathmandu, Nepal
Phone: 01-4492904
www.maitinepal.org
Maiti Nepal is an organization dedicated to the prevention of trafficking Nepali girls for prostitution and other forms of forced labor, through intervention and legal advocacy.

**OSCE [Organization for Security and Co-operation in Europe]**
www.osce.org/cthb
Wallnerstrasse 6
1010 Vienna
Austria
Tel: +43 1 514 36 6000
Fax: +43 1 514 36 6996
The OSCE is the world's largest regional security organization whose 56 participating States span the geographical area from Vancouver to Vladivostok.

**Kids Help Phone (Canada)**
Toll-free: 1-800-668-6868
Canada's only toll-free national hotline for children and youth. Bilingual (English and French).

**Muslim Women's Help Line (U.K.)**
Hotline: 0181 904 8193 or 0181 908 6715
Hotline for Muslim women and girls in the U.K. dealing with domestic violence, sexual abuse, and other problems.

**Action on Elder Abuse (U.K.)**
Freephone: 0808 808 8141
www.elderabuse.org.uk

**National Domestic Violence Hotline (Canada)**
Toll-free: 1-800-363-9010
All provinces. Bilingual (English and French).

**National Eating Disorders Information Centre (Canada)**
Toll-free: 1-866-633-4220

**Nottelefon Zurich**
Phone: 01-291 46 46
www.frauenberatung.ch
(Pages available in German, English, French, Spanish & Italian) Counseling by phone and in person, free referrals to doctors and legal advisors, for women dealing with sexual harassment or abuse, or exploitation by therapists, doctors, ministers, at work or home.

**Women's Aid Federation of England**
Freephone: 0808 2000 247
www.womensaid.org.uk
Free, 24-hour helpline for domestic violence victims. Support and information, referrals to refuges, counseling, and services for children

IF THIS BOOK HELPED YOU, I WOULD LOVE TO HEAR FROM YOU AT
ROOSTERSCAGE@OUTLOOK.COM